Nothing Left to Lose

Natasha Head

Winter Goose
Publishing

Winter Goose Publishing
2701 Del Paso Road, 130-92
Sacramento, CA 95835

www.wintergoosepublishing.com
Contact Information: info@wintergoosepublishing.com

Nothing Left to Lose
COPYRIGHT © 2012 by Natasha Head

First Edition, March, 2012
ISBN: 978-0-9851548-1-3

Cover Art by Winter Goose Publishing
Typeset by Victoriakumar Yallamelli

Published in the United States of America

Dedication

My dearest family, without you, this would have never come to be. I thank you for your encouragement, your support, and your faith in my passion.

To all the poets who have found the courage to share your words, and in turn, your heart and soul with me, YOU are my inspiration. Your unwavering encouragement has been the strength I needed to find my own courage to share my words, my struggles, and my heart.

Introduction

I have been writing poetry since the age of ten, when my father presented me with a journal for my birthday. It was beautiful, with soft pink pages, lined in burgundy script, with a stunning silk cover. Even at that age, I knew it was too beautiful a creation to be filled with the typical ramblings of the ten-year-old mind . . . so I wrote a poem.

Since then, I have relied upon pen and prose to battle the ugliness that seems to pervade the real world. The only reprieve I know is when I can sit, with pen and notebook in hand, and write until that constant white noise finally settles.

This longed-for silence, this ability to work through the madness . . . is available to all.

Poetry is not reserved for the select few, it is not elitist, it does not care who you are or where you came from, or judge you for the mistakes you have made. It speaks to all, for all, and is able to reflect back to us, through the art of language, an image of the world that is real, that is now.

Poetry is the pulse of humanity. It always has been, throughout our histories. Every heart carries the burden of the poem waiting to be written, a hurt that needs healing, a mistake that needs forgiving, a love that deserves reward.

It is my hope that by sharing this collection with you, of my own trials and tribulations, my own hopes and dreams, that I might perhaps be able to convince you to grab a pen, and write the story your own heart wants to tell, and lend your own voice to the chorus of poets and writers who are doing the same.

The pen has always been said to be mightier than the sword, and our world is in need of a different sort of army. It is our responsibility, as global citizens, to recognize the need and to act . . . to bear witness to our Poetic Evolution.

Power to the Poets.

Table of Contents

Static {stat-ic}: lacking movement, development or vitality

Static

Trapped between what was, what
is . . . no movement; fear
holds me motionless.

All directions equal no choice, as
fear gives way to chaos . . .
enslavement.

What needs to be done, I
don't want to do, my thoughts
constant, my nightmares

real, feeling force, breaking
pressure, resisting to the point
of stagnation.

Safety Zone

She likes to hide
away from prying eyes,
where there is no judgement,
no condemnation.
Where she can simply be
left alone to fester
without pretense,
without show.
No bragging rights required.

Where no one notices
the lack of a smile,
the missing twinkle
in once happy eyes.
She just wants to fall
into her self-imposed abyss.
Simply losing herself
to the gray.

Looking Back

Life was once vibrant
with no cause for concern.
We danced a rainbow of color
with no reason to fear the shadow.

They were there, lurking.
Patiently waiting
for us to turn from the light,
to acknowledge their presence.

Knowing we would
because we always do.
Such is the nature
of fools like us.

On a forgettable afternoon,
caught up in the color,
I turned to the shadow,
setting it free.

Before I could think twice,
before I recognized the need
to call on the light,
we were swimming amongst them.

The need, fast becoming strength,
to keep our heads above
the murky infested waters
from which they were born.

Tea With the Tax Lady

She sits at my table; prim, proper.
I sit beside her covered
in black fondant, aiming to please

my daughter for her ninth birthday. She
is quiet, knowing. Having spent
the past two weeks reviewing,

auditing, correcting amateur ledgers,
bank statements. All responsibility on me.
All embarrassment, on me.

She shuffles papers, smiles and pulls
out a legal-sized folder, a pile of documents
requiring signatures. My signatures.

Still smiling, she hands me the pen.
Page after page, X after X.
No explanation, as though she knows.

I know it wouldn't matter anyway.
I sign, and sign, and sign, and
sign right here on the dotted line.

After errors and penalties
and mistakes and late fees, I see
the cloud of hope that was to get us through

evaporate in a wash of now-dead trees.
And still she smiles, as she neatly pulls the paper
back to her patent-leather attaché case.

Rising, still smiling. I now understand
the smile is condescending . . .
"Bet you'll think twice
before going into business for yourself again."

Dogma

They stroll these streets
branded as different,
though they are the original.
Off-color remarks
need not be spoken quietly.
They know their place.
1000 fenced acres,
while we eat the land of their ancestors,
crossing streets
to avoid eye contact.
We convince ourselves
it is not the guilt
of hundreds of years
of oppression.
Barging in,
we laid claim to their future,
wondering why
they hate us so.
Wounds that have bled
through centuries.
Tainting the waters of our river.
Muddied by the blood of innocents.
It will never again
run clear.

IV

Support?
I question the word,
let alone your intention.
Words?
My religion,
turned to sulphur

on your blasphemous tongue.
Gripping my heart,
constant stagnation.

No evolution.
Just revolution.
When I simply craved . . .

a renaissance.

I Prefer the Silence

When the awkward silence becomes the norm,
when it becomes comfortable
to the point you prefer it,
this is when the idea of "better"
becomes much like a dream
remembered six hours
into a fourteen-hour workday.
And you know you crave something;
pizza, chocolate
doesn't quite cut it.
But you know
you have a need to feed.
It is your soul that's hungry
and you don't know how to fill it.
The dreams.
The hopes.
The promise of better?
We have already established
all that was lost,
suffocated by the weight
of the awkward silence.

The Grind

Maddening . . . so maddening!
This quest for peace.
Mind-quiet.

To be taken in offence.
An act against this beast
we have sacrificed our entire lives for.

Frustration mounts, work through,
pounding headache, upset
stomach, ulcer bleeds.

This is madness.
Complete and perfect.
There is no escape.

Travel Unintended

I read of poems written
The beauty of the world
Exotic, foreign
Customs, cultures

I wonder
Should I ever be so blessed
To write from such a space
Inspired

I start to notice
Where my own pen has traveled
Rolling fields of green
Giant, sleeping mountains

Alive with fire
On an autumn afternoon
The clash of the blue
With the brown

As opposite shores
Battle for attention
The varied accents
Different at every quick-way

A colorful folktale
To explain the magic of each place
Wrapped in lore and ritual
Fantasy and faith

My Nova Scotia

My home
How could I leave her
With so many roads left to explore?

Chore List

Spit, shine, polish.
Makes no dent.
In a house that has stood

for one hundred years or more.
Where there is always dust.
Always dirt.

And perhaps worst of all,
there is always the aroma,
of something that is not yours.

Ransomed

I was fickle with my freedom.
Thought it something I deserved.
Never believed
anyone could strip it away.
Caged now.
Like a beast, unruly.
Spirit broken.
At the mercy of *The Man*.

Nuclear Air

It's amazing to realize just how quickly
we come to possess a space.
To contaminate even the air.
When others visit,
inhale our poison,
do we then possess them, too?
Nothing is sacred in nuclear air.
The chance to survive, to become more,
somehow bigger, better
than anything to be imagined.
All we have is our imagination, after all.
And when you come to know
just how quickly you can invade a space,
you then come to know
your power.

Death of a Poet

The Poet drowns
Lost amongst the pile of paperwork
Gasping for air in a sea of gossip
Overflowing water cooler
Sitcom cliché

Festering, simmering,
Skin peeling, acid drenched
Born to strip your bones
Birthing pressure
Craving soul

Productivity, production
The poet struggles to hang on
To identity, alphabetized
In manila folders, hard copy

Voice is lost
Amongst a digital symphony
Phones, printers, faxes
White noise corruption

Such is the life
The Poet ingests
To provide for the others
Who shall remain nameless.

Frozen

I have seen a life laid to waste,
in the name of pure stubbornness,
in the absolute definition of denial.

I see my own life.
Caught up on the same rails,
charging full steam ahead,
to a tunnel where no light shines.

The gates of experience fly by.
Still-frames of adventures
I have excused myself from
for reasons, for selfishness.

Vanity . . . shame.
The double yellow line,
solid and illuminated,
laughs as I attempt to find the nerve.

To dare cross.
Throwing up walls of resistance
as the hourglass bleeds
grains of sand I can't afford.

I have seen a lifetime
laid to waste,
and in its shadow,
I have seen my own.

Rat Race

I exist within a world
of stolen conversations
overheard in lineups
for coffee and cigarettes.

Double milk, king-size please.
A single sugar to offset bitterness,
and a silent prayer for Maggie
who's been laid up all summer long.

Nursing the broken ankle received
climbing the mount in . . .
I like to think it was the Himalayas.

But I miss the last few words
as I step to grab my coffee.

Exit Through the Front

We will exit through the front
So everyone will know
We made the choice to walk away
We chose to let it go

We will exit through the front
To show we're not ashamed
To leave these trappings all behind
There's more to life than fame

We will exit through the front
So others know they're not alone
We made the choice to leave this way
We know a house is not a home

Bittersweet Victory

We have survived!
For better or for worse
we escaped
with even a bit of dignity
left intact.
With no bold notice
on our beautiful door.
A sin really,
that the beautiful life
forgot we were part of it.
The penalty for impersonating
one of its own
was much steeper than we
could have imagined.

Momentum {moh-men-t*uh*m}: force or speed of movement

Momentum

Direction chosen.
Courage suddenly
and without warning,
discovered.

Letting go, moving forward.
Mourning not the loss,
rather celebrating
new beginnings.

A fresh start, a lower rung.
Dues still to pay,
but out from under
there is air to breathe.

If

If you're going to write the words,
make them count.

Write with courage.
With no fear, no censorship.

Write with wild abandon.
Own the original thought.

Tell your story, speak your tale.
Control the ink that bleeds from the wounds

yesterday's shrapnel has left to scar.

She Runs

She runs
Hiding behind the heart
They all know is sensitive
Trying to live up to expectations
To be the woman she never wanted to be
If it means they will be happy
She figures the cost
Is worth it
But
Sometimes, when alone
She works up the nerve to wonder
To question
Why her own happiness
Is never mentioned
Or considered worth fighting for
And she is angry
And in her anger
There is power
And a shift is made
A goal is set
Tunnel vision required
There will be casualties

Acceptance

Is this how the world rewards you,
for having the courage to chase your dream?
By ripping the very idea of security
out from under.
By stripping the very values you consider truth—
until they are torn beyond recognition?
By instilling such a fear of the system
burrowing into your brain
that you make the decision
to exist well below ground
as the real you, the system rejected?

Reflection

How is it we are so easily convinced
to chase another's dream at the cost
of sacrificing our own?
How do they manipulate our minds,
convince us it's our dream too?
Egging us on with dancing, golden carrots
and a treasure chest of rewards
that never come to fruition.
I know you know what I speak of.
I know you, too, have sacrificed,
past the attempts
to end original thought.
I know you feel it
on those nights when sleep only teases
and you find yourself staring down a stranger
trapped in the reflection of a spotted bathroom mirror.
Staring into deadened eyes,
no longer recognizing.
Wondering,
"What the hell?"

Clean Slate

To be alone with these thoughts
Overwhelming
Heavy burdens upon a heart

That can no longer bear their weight
To throw hands in the air
Admit defeat

In the face of the biggest beast
I have yet to battle
Always fighting

But now comes the time
For letting go, for there is nothing of me
Left for them to take

The Wood Pile

It would loom massive before us.
Teasing , taunting.
But we would take it on
stick after stick,
building character
with bruises and battered fingernails.
The trophies to prove it.

But once stacked,
the best hiding spot in the world
was the reward.
Never mind the spiders
or the flat-backed potato bugs,
nor the worms that would
slither their way into conversations.

Once we were done building character
we got to build worlds
and conquer kingdoms
behind the wood pile.

Empathy

I know you hurt
I know because I have felt it too
When hope is lost
When light becomes the enemy
And suddenly shadows welcome
When they used to make you run

I know it pains
Physically on a level
No other understands
I know the heaviness
Of your bones
Your heart
Your head
And I know
There's nothing I can do
To make it better

Realization

It was never something I meant to do.
In between being ignored,
being taken advantage of,
it just sort of happened.

A chance conversation
suddenly woke me up,
made me realize
it's been this way.

Because I have allowed it to be.
I have the power.
I can act on the power.
I can begin to move.

Core

Oh you fools, can you not see?
You're doomed to repeat history.
The fruit you harvest from not your tree
was spoiled young, in infancy!

From archaic truths you live a lie,
forgetting that your god has died.
A life of pain you pass to us,
corrupted bloodline, broken trust.

To run from you, I think we must.
Our lives you covet, unbridled lust.
As you boast of sacrifice
you deny the toil, the strife.

We stay to watch your body break.
The child's future you will forsake,
as you insist on proving worth.
Raising Cain, your daughter's birth.

Leaving mess for those left behind.
Believing the lies you've told your mind.
Oh, you fools, can you not see,
you've chosen to write MY history,

with this fruit from another's tree.
A poisoned apple . . . just for me.

Master of Manipulation

He is master
I am slave
Under his orders only
Do I open

The constant
And loyal companion
The friend who tells no secrets
Though I know each and every one

Some may think this codependent
But he brings only my best
I swallow his worst

It can hurt to be loved so hard

I will remain his confident
His mistress
His friend
Every evening

I will give of myself
A crisp, clean page
So that he can bleed

Unto me
I will not judge
Nor will I talk back
And with his sword

He will eat of my flesh

Scar my insides
And always
Feel better when done

Oh yes, it hurts so good
To be loved so hard

Collusion

An extension of myself
Mockingly staring back
Reminding me of what
I once might have been
Like the private places of my mind
Her floors are littered
With tokens of lack
Scarcity
Uncaring hands
Leave fingerprints upon her walls
Pointing out her imperfections
A reflection of her inner self
Manipulating, forcing control
Set brightly on display
For the world to see
But I'm the only one that knows
That girl is not me

Back Road Consequences

Secrets live down dark dirt roads,
that neighbors try to hide.
Pay no mind to what others do
so it's easy to choose sides.

Secluded amongst the evergreens,
miles from their friends.
Where privacy and quietness
would cover up their sins.

Underground they traded well.
Thought they knew the risks.
Through the woods they quickly came,
silent amongst the mist.

A hidden drive, ravine in back
would not let them run,
when they realized a friendly knock
was hiding a loaded gun.

Days would pass before someone
finally risked a glance,
down private lane to locked up house.
Through the windows, nervous stance.

Through dirty panes and spotted glass
the damage could be seen.
The blood, the bodies, the starving dogs.
Such a sight obscene.

They made the news reporters come,
but within a day or two,
back to normal, back to secrets.
Back to what they do.

Manifest

These fickle fascinations
That only serve to distract
Hiding true purpose
Suspending passion
With oddity and flair
Overwhelming the senses
Silencing myth
With ancient magic
To invoke
Bombarded by mass consciousness
Demanding from ourselves
That which was never desired
Fighting the program
Resisting the system
Becoming that which is most feared
A creator
Of original thought

School Girl

Long live the squiggly script
of the heart-sick school girl.
Dotting *i*'s with gilded hearts.
Practicing the autograph
until it is red carpet worthy.
Daring to dream of better tomorrows.
Sincere in her belief
in the goodness of all.
Pray she never loses
that naivety.
Pray you never doubt
her innocence.
And always have faith
in the good.

By All Means Necessary

Like the sun, I rise.
Stepping into a sea of responsibility.
Overwhelmed, but smiling.
Like what is expected.
I face the day in denial
of the fear that has taken residence.
Seeping through the affirmations
I have used to manipulate my mind.

This is life.
By all means necessary.

I go through the motions.
A brief reprieve of routine,
before the bombardment begins.
Taking it on the chin.
Putting out fires.
Smothering in their smoke.

This is life.
By all means necessary.

Reacting, reacting, reacting.
Solving problems, then solving more.
Keeping it all together.
The age old question:
power or force?
All done with a smile.

This is life.
By all means necessary.

A Conversation

Can I be honest with you?
Can I tell you how much I DON'T want this to happen?
I know it has to,
even though knowing doesn't make it hurt any less.

Would you be honest with me?
Will you allow your heart to speak?
Will you tell me what I hope to hear,
even though every cell within your rational mind screams against it?

Will we make it through this?
I need to hear we will, even if you think differently.
Will you lie to me, out of love?
I promise to not hold it against you.

Poetic Eyes

The poetic landscape
Invites tired eyes
When you define the world
With poetry
All chaos
Finds its place
And suddenly sense is recognized
Pain as muse
Out of which realization dawns
Hurt
Suddenly lives and breathes
Alive in words
The beauty of emotion
Love . . . or lack of
Pleads to be written
Forever chronicled
In the untainted chambers
Of a broken heart
All that is
All that ever was
Bleeds poetically
In a red too brilliant
For words

Evolution {ev-*uh*-loo-sh*uh*n}: any process of formation or growth and development.

Life Sucks

We've heard it one thousand times and more.
Life's hard, life's not fair, life's not supposed to be this way.
Life sucks!

We've heard it shouted out windows and thrown out the doors.
Life's a bitch, don't dream your life away, life is about hard work.
Life sucks!

If we just keep on yelling, saying it more.
I wasn't supposed to turn out this way! This wasn't my plan!
Life sucks!
Ah yes . . . such is life, but
if it didn't sometimes suck
would it be easier to appreciate
those moments when it doesn't?

A sunrise on an October morn, the cry of your daughter's first new-
born?
The song of the loon, lost in the mist, the feel of your husband's very
first kiss?
A stream in the forest, crystal and pure, grand adventures and stories,
mythic folklore?

If life didn't suck, at least once in a while,
wouldn't it be that much harder to smile?

Yeah, life sucks! So what!
Doesn't make it any less worth living.

Creators...

Creators take charge!
Account for these beasts
who own the shadows we've allowed to invade
our gentle lands.
Blocking our light,
we have let ourselves cower
thinking we've no other choice
but to let them rule our minds.
Sharpened pencils stab our hearts
calling our earnings their own,
feasting upon the harvest
of those less fortunate.

Creators take charge!
This world is ours to empower!
The powers that be,
we permit to be.
Take back your power!
Raise your voice to be heard!
It is our truth, our dignity,
that will pay the price.
You are worth
so much more than they have led you to believe.
You are loved
so much more than you know!

Creators take charge!
Own your magnificent power.
Let the light they have tried to smother
shine bright enough for all.
Allow yourselves to become

the glorious gods and goddesses
you have forgotten you have always been.
Throughout all our shared eternities
you are divinity manifested
within this earthly realm.
You are, within yourself,
the miracle you have been waiting for.

Back to Darkness

For eons now the beast has been fought,
killing sin with light,
but shadows grow and now are caught,
no longer worth the fight.
To force a person to change the tide,
deny thy inner self,
emotions raging, overflow the cup,
darkness is true wealth.

Come on to me and let me be,
all I've always dreamed.
Don't mind the smile, it's painted on,
not always as it seems.
Don't mind the cross, it decorates,
adorning swollen chest.
Don't mind the air of confidence,
I'm no better than the rest.

Let go my hand and let me rise,
stop holding on so tight.
I belong to no one but
the darkness of the night.
So steal the sun and with it run,
without it shadows die.
No more pretending all is good
within this web of lies.

I am here just as I am
and I'm so sick of trying.
To be so much unlike I thought I was
is damn near terrifying.

So back to darkness I must go,
it's where I found true love.
A pen and paper . . . all alone,
it fits me like a glove.

Business Head

What is this world of business
where friendships are destroyed,
relationships ruined,
families torn apart,
all for the sake of a dollar?
What is this world of business,
where the contracts are only as solid
as the people doing the signing,
and if they have a lawyer on payroll,
you don't stand a chance?
What is this world of business
that takes your values,
steals your morals,
and rapes your truth
in exchange for success?

This is the way of the world!
they explain,
as my quality of life suffers.
You're too soft!
I feel myself shrink, my heart wilt.
Ultimately it's the heart I must live with,
and unlike the head,
I cannot manipulate it
to accept these ways
of business.

Bring YOU

Let go of your dictionary
And your Harvard mind
The words couldn't care less
Just write them
Feel their simplicity
Feel their power
No wonder they overwhelm the form

Hearts are easy
Easy to love, easy to break
Easy only has two syllables

Speak to me honestly
You need not hide behind
All these things everyone
Convinced you
That you wanted

I am here like you
Broken, battered
Scarred from the battle
But far from beaten

Talk to me like you mean it
Speak to us in truth
So we can feel the words
You've been fighting to say

We couldn't make it any easier
Just bring you

Secret

I am in here you know
Despite these walls I've been forced to build
To guarantee my survival
I am still here
Whole
In tact
Finding the courage
To share my tale

Mom's Supper

Tonight we break bread
over old fashioned favorites.
This ever shrinking world
sometimes allows us to forget
slow roasted turkey,
buttered and crisped, salt and pepper
to season.
Turnips,
mashed and extra sweet.
Local, from the garden carrots.
Real butter melting, glistening.
All swimming
in Mom's gravy.
With a mountain of fresh mashed potatoes
standing guard.

Tangled Webs

So tell me little one,
what makes you so bold
as to think I will allow
you to invade my empire
and remain as king?

The sunbeams trapped within your motive
almost fool me into thinking
you are one with us.
Creating beauty,
Shaping form.

But all too soon we are caught
spellbound by your ploy,
and wrapped too tight to breathe . . .

Oh no, kind sir.
I know your type, you need to feed.
It's my broom for you!

This Voice

Does this voice that speaks,
through cheap pens
bought in bulk,

inspire, delight, sadden,
enlighten? Does this voice
that speaks in faded ink,

broken words, stutter,
like the dry point desperate
to be filled?

Motivated, inspired.
Does this voice speak
loud enough to be heard?

Beyond the tattered borders
of these pages?

Quantum Heart

My world I have created
By mere existence within your dimension
You were nothing more

Than an unformed wave
On a sea of potentiality
Until I chose

To collapse you on my shore
Where sand castles are golden
Housing treasures beyond dreams

And the waves collapse true blue
Lost beneath pure indigo sky
How I wished across this potential sea
For you to ride your wave to me

Paper Lanterns

Paper lanterns decorate
Secret paths
Hidden even in the brilliance of the sun
This night we will speak of mysteries
Our missing pieces finally found
In the midst of the magic
That is connection
For so long we have known
We have been so close
Always searching
Overlooking
Seeking that one set of eyes
That refuse to turn from our heated gaze
These paper lanterns
The only totems
To mark our presence . . .
To honor us found

One Love

Why do we let these borders divide us,
shape us, mold us, somehow define us?
We need not be held by invisible lines.
We must overcome, a sign of our times.
Since birth and beyond, we are all the same.
No matter our color, religion or name.
We worship our gods, we all bleed blood-red.
We live every day knowing end results dead.
We all carry our burdens, we all hurt inside.
We covet our houses, where our hearts abide.
We are shaped by our family and cursed by the same.
We all have our demons we struggle to tame.
Know when you see me,
you see you, too.
And show me the best
on the inside of you.
When I look in your eyes,
all that I see,
reflecting back,
is an image of me.
This is how close we really are,
no matter our histories, or many scars.

My Nature

Speak to the earth and it shall teach thee
Of hope, of pain, of love and joy
Birth and rebirth, cause, effect
She knows all your secrets
Yet dares not speak them
She is Mother
Protector
She is
All

Common Man

The common man walks with a burden
Some might call it his thinking mind
Morals, instinct, know no place
In animal kingdoms
Survival the name
Sick, twisted game
Such is this
We call
Life

Harvest

The seed sprouts slowly.
Buried deep
amongst the soft tissue
of an alternate reality
yet to be born.
Reaching limbs it takes hold
until suddenly rooted.
Solid.
Grasped and understood,
it is acted upon.
Moving from the realm of idea
to the matrix of creation,
where it will be allowed to grow,
nurtured by the hands
of the thinker.

Divination

Stones cast are revealed
Through the dust and ether futures
Caught on winds of change

Picnic

They are seen
Tiny
Stick-like

Dancing in the sun spots
As the breeze
Ripples across the water

Their laughter
Carries up river
Where we

Have tried to isolate ourselves
They play
On a greener grass while

We tiptoe over
Ancient and exposed
Roots of the towering pine

We have chosen as our defense

Prophecy

Dancing like the fool of Waite
Towards an unseen edge
The universal cliff

While man's best friend
Nips at his heels but
Eyes to the sky

The nipping becomes
Nuisance and he
Trains his brain to ignore

All he owns
A burden upon his back
Top heavy

Gravity laughs last as
He blindly stumbles never to
Regain his footing

Angst

Why must I fight so to write these words?
Why must you question their merit?
That I want to write them should be enough.

Though no dollars will they earn, of them I freely give.
Why is it you value
only the dollars and not their message?

Does not a sincere smile hold some value?
Is there not worth in heart content?
Worth beyond your bag of coins?

These words will live on long after I've gone to dust.
Can you say the same
of your dollars?

Rule Book

Who has put these conditions, these rules,
on something as grand as love?
How does one tell a heart to behave
when it beats on a vibration higher than the mind?

Who is so bold as to try to shrink this emotion?
Constricting the heart, allowing room for one,
only one?
This is not the love my heart knows.

My heart cries out in anger for these troubled times
that our minds have forced upon us,
as we try our hardest to follow the rules of love
that leave bodies on the roadside.

Uncared for, deprived.
For the world would not let us welcome them,
as our hearts were already occupied,
and we know there's only room for one.

I am regarded with angry, disbelieving eyes,
for passing along small tokens of care
to those who have been classed unworthy.
But my heart will mend, for I know the secret . . .

all we are is love.

Dreamscape

Awash in indigo
Bathed in alien light
For there is no source to be found
A soundtrack of silence
Breath shallow
Miscounted
As drops of paisley dance
Falling against
The backdrop of the universe
I slip deeper
Carried in a cloud
Of unconsciousness
For once
Light as a feather
As there are no earthly trinkets
To hold me ensnared
I have found the road to freedom
Where I need not hate myself
Based on obligations unfulfilled
No one needs me here
They are merely
Happy to have me

Human

There is a sense of comfort
you become accustomed to
to the point of complacency.
You count on the goodness
of human kind.
You believe it is good.
You expect it—then take advantage,
but evil is born in the hearts of men.
Planted next to love,
it grows in hearts and minds,
rallying behind holy words,
protecting holy lands,
convincing their hearts
they fight for gods,
and soon blood spills.
Empires topple.
Glass houses,
decorated in superiority,
become the slivers of swords
that pierce our existence.

I Pray

I pray for change every day,
but don't consider myself
wise enough to know
how to bring it about.

We are all so very broken.
My heart hurts,
my stomach tightens,
blood pressure rises.

Fear can do that
to a person,
to a country,
to a world.

Fair Warning

From merely observation, to engagement,
the sense of being stared at
is now known as fact.
The envelope was simple,
the paper just the same,
but written in a muddy ink
was just one word—my name.
I know too many secrets,
have kept them all these years,
when I could have told.
I could have run.
But we agreed, you see,
that it would be better
to just let it be.
Rumors of his return,
but never dreamed he'd dare
to go to such a sick degree
so I would know he's watching me.

Aging Ways

It seems the days grow longer now
despite an earlier setting sun.
I've not the time for the foolishness,
like I used to.
Perhaps that is what is most unnerving.

I spotted a tree on the roadside yesterday,
as we travelled through the valley.
Already the brilliant green
was being overtaken.
Sacrificed to the raging red of autumn fire.

Life's like that, you know.
Slipping away so easily
as we count the moments wasted.
And all we've never done . . .
another blank in my notebook of dreams.

It can steal from you if you let it.
Weighing you down with imagined obligations.
Living for another is no good
if it has caused you to sacrifice yourself.
Your hopes and dreams have to matter too . . .

I often wonder if things would have been different
if I hadn't stumbled through so blindly
in an effort to please all but me.
To this day, no one can tell me how to live with the guilt.

That comes with doing for yourself . . .
after all, isn't life about sacrifice?

To be rewarded at the pearly gates
with eternity upon a gilded throne?

Afraid I still have way too much living to do
to accept that.
Afraid I have to start,
doing it for me.

Smells Like November

Car exhaust fogs up the drive
Its aroma thick
Cloying, like steam from a kettle

But cold, unforgiving
The frost melts, trickling
Down windshield, freezing again

Half-drip, poetic patterns
Colliding, dividing, teeth
Chatter, news announcer

Warns of more to come
Burnt umber leaves crunch
Beneath the all-seasons, left

To drop from skeletal limbs
Drifting through the void of
The seasons, reminders

And below the frost
Amongst exhaust
It smells like November

Change

Change . . . thrives and breathes on the wind,
and like the fiery autumn leaf
unknowingly let go,
it seldom rests in one spot too long.

Change . . . is ever constant.
Through the seasons, the turn of the wheel,
like Maritime weather
at the mercy of our great mother.

Change . . . makes room for bigger, better.
The cutting away of the old, tired, used.
Returning to the Earth, so that a new seed
may sprout and grow from its remnants.

Change . . . an evolution of spirit.
Where bands of eternity wrap
'round the ether of the soul,
forever searching, never knowing.

Change . . . the mystery of unknown.
The adventure of untraveled.
The fear of never before.
The fuel that drives.

Ambition, passion, hatred, love,
growth, sustenance, nourishment,
death, loss, sorrow, pain.
Letting go, letting God, letting you.

Grass Fire

Grassroots ignited
leaders stand, frightened
as the masses loom up to fend

or defend as the case may be
the simplicity of you and me
human nature looms

the voice of doom
predicts demise
as foundations of democracy shake

quake upon the trading floors
the land of prosperity
shall be no more

as houses, once homes
begin to decay
welcome to the Capitalist way

where the rich get richer
and the con man will thrive
while we are left hungry—without alibi

and if we turn to THEM
in hopes we'll survive,
than freedom means nothing

and will soon surely die.

The Unsung Song

Histories are forever waiting to be written
by the victors of battles waged.
Steal the pen to salute the one
who has the song
to yet be sung.

Warriors are forever ready to do battle.
War painted like Picasso,
fighting through Cubism
when he had the song
to yet be sung.

Women are forever ready to love,
and sometimes don't survive it.
Hoping only to tell the tale,
the melody of a song
yet to be sung.

Men forever fumble to protect
in haste, but so endearing.
Their Picasso war paint smeared
in their hurry to sing the song
that has not yet been sung.

The Earth cries out in anger
against the abuse
our mere existence brings.
And thus brings forth the starting note,
of the song that has yet to be sung.

The Village

Through shanties and unkempt vessels
Seasoned now from lack of use
Grey and weathered
With no shine left to shimmer
Just the glimpse of a forgotten name
In the haze of a midsummer afternoon
Once worthy, now forgotten
Save for a few dusty shelves
Holding her post cards in once prosperous drug stores
Not that long ago
They would celebrate
And feast upon her return
Traps . . . like so many forgotten ghosts
Decorate the homesteads of men
Who were once called captain
Now painted in colors
Gaudy and overstated
Like men who would woo Shakespeare
On a stage where the feminine would be mocked
Now reserved for photo ops
In seasonal gift shops
Lawn ornaments
For those who have left for greener seas
Of currency and neon lights
But Mum and Pop remain
Tending to gardens of granite
From rocking chairs on unsteady verandas
Overlooking the blue
They chose to hang their hat on.

All That Glitters

All that glitters is not gold.
Sometimes it's hot pink against a backdrop of concrete
where wilted weeds fight to break through cracks,
and a chewing gum wrapper meets its fate, ensnared.
Sometimes it's a balloon, deflated, denying itself.
Weighted down by the water of worry.
What goes up, must come down,
but you can't be afraid to fly.
Sometimes, it's a lemon-drop lollypop
sparkling in the hand of a diabetic.
Sugar-rush suicide.
But the laws of what is remain,
and the temptation to defy gravity
leaves only the weighted balloon,
for the weeds to entangle.

Red Tape

Drowning in the bureaucracy
Ruled by those who have never done
This task has become cumbersome
But doomed, this is reality

Paper high as the eye can see
A daunting task that can't be won
Drowning in the bureaucracy
Ruled by those who have never done

Sign a contract and kill a tree
Never replant a single one
But that's okay; it's how it's done
We are quite important, you see
Drowning in the bureaucracy

To the Paper

There is another version of myself that I don't show the world, for fear
that they will run from me . . .
I'm not a normal girl.
Longing for acceptance, I wear the face I must,
and to the paper I escape, before the real me rusts.

There is truth within my pen yet I'm too afraid to share.
Unless I hide between the lines and act like I don't care.
With easy words I build my mask that hides my secret smile,
and hope between the lines you'll stay with me but for a while.

To the paper I must run when my facade starts to break down.
When this world has beaten me and turned my truth around.
When my pen just wants to bleed, a vein straight from my heart.
When my life spills forth, line by line, each word ripping me apart.

To the paper where I share the thoughts I don't dare say.
It's the blanket where I have let my troubles simply lay.
It's the shoulder that I need on days I have to cry.
It's the real me that you'll find, hidden between these lines.

It's where I find my sanity when I start to doubt
that in this world I'll never really figure it all out.
It's where I love, it's where I live, it's all I really need.
It's to that paper that I run when my pen starts to bleed.

It is my church where I am able to speak with the divine.
And if you really want to know me just read between the lines.

NWCU

We have floundered in a sea of plastic waves for far too long.
Synthetic promises, digitally manipulated
as the maggots squirm through the pathways,
feeding on the seeds of dreams we dare to dream.

Planted within our minds for the sole survival of the corporation.
These beasts that rule our bordered nations.
Profits foster discrimination.
Bloody, permanent, mutilation.

Dead to the sensitivities that one time breathed life.
The maggots devour,
all in the name of the bull and the bear.
Driving dollars, sacrificing individuality,
regurgitating dogma.

Pushed through classrooms and kindergartens,
church basements and town halls.
It is the violent and inhumane assassination
of the mind of freethinking man.

It is the death of faith, of hope, the belief that we can . . .
We don't have to, now that life is plastic,
and on the maggots march,
devouring our resources.

On the orders of the ones we chose to give them.
The same voices we bow to when commanded.
The same voices that have tried to end,
This New World Creative Union.

The Other

She looks around the tiny room.
Dark—though she knows outside,
the high noon sun

burns like a bullet
descending upon the concrete.
Sparse . . . nothing more,

than a table at her only window
and a chair, straight-backed, hard,
uninviting.

Her view? A string of ancient fruit-of-the-looms
flapping in the hot breeze
like a flag for the defeat they represent.

Never to be white again,
no matter how many rocks they are
beaten against,

in this modern and forgotten jungle.
A bed, more like a cot
from an episode of *MASH*,

greets her tired and weary body.
Here she will lie
when the words finally refuse to come.

But for now, hers is a story that needs telling.
And she will write . . .
write . . . write . . .

For now content to watch over her shoulder,
until the eternal sleep
finally calls her home.

Inevitable

The monsters win
because we let them.
A beast that thrives
on scarcity
cannot help but be held accountable
to the basic rules of supply and demand.
When you feed on profits,
gain sustenance from values,
starvation comes
only when demand drops.
It may be the beast that holds the rations,
but it is us who dictates demand.
Burn, baby, BURN!
Complaining
while we step to the cross willingly,
with no hope of resurrection.

In Your Face

To find the courage to share.
To lift these words
from sun-bleached pages
through cob webs of doubt.

To find the nerve.
Who does she think she is,
to speak in such a manner,
to cast shadows upon?

The light that shines,
just bright enough to blind.
Who is she to question
the status quo?

How dare she
attempt to pry open
unwilling eyes
that are content to stay unseeing!

To find the courage,
despite it all . . .
I guess you could say,
I'm the girl with the pen.

Think About It

So tell me . . . whose life have you been living?

Could we take a moment . . . perhaps strip away
the dogma that has been taught to you?
Force fed on spoons and forks

that have never once left your mouth.
Who are you, I ask, and without thought,
like a perfectly timed reaction,

you toss me a name. If it is unique
to who you are, then yes, perhaps
you are truly special. I prefer to see it

as the first attack. Who named you?

And who named this religion that
has shaped more than just your Sunday mornings?
I challenge you now, really let go,

and let God. Not by Constantine's definition,
look beyond the Eye of Horus
to the divinity that was born

when you were. Already known,
forced to be forgotten at the hands
of agenda driven politicians

who planted the seemingly innocent mustard seed.

Let us look now, to every bit of history

that came through textbooks developed
by the man with the plan.

Every bias, every fear
fabricated to ensure complacency.
Every discipline issue, learning problem.

Medicated to breed foot soldiers,
beaten down based on social status
placed on you by a fifty-year-old primary teacher

whose only mission is to break you.

How much of who you are is based
on the village, the country you call home?
The teachers, the doctors, the friends

who make you feel less for your art?
Who brands you as odd because you
brave original thought?

Every prescription granted to quell your uniqueness.
To make you fit better, to help you feel
normal. To better assign you to a worthwhile position

within societal ranks . . . one where you won't hurt yourself.

And what of these rulers who expect you
to believe all they do is for you? While they replace
the batteries on the strings they use

to police the you that you seem to think you are.
This "government" who knows you better than anyone
based on status, income, geography, kin;

defining your usefulness, your contribution to a cause
you never knew you were marching for. Creating war
to keep you working, while lining silken pockets.

One new fee, one new tax, one new devil at a time.

But don't forget . . . you've got their god on your side.
Now let's have some real fun,
let's take away the borders . . .

restrictions based on conscription,
invisible trade barriers control your movements indefinitely,
ready with a whole new name for you

if you dare to cross the line. Ah, freedom,
a wonderful thing to cherish.
Shall we take this experiment to the world?

Imagine we have all stripped away the trappings
of this supposed civilized society.
And let us look now to our true brothers and sisters.

Nameless, egoless, penniless and with no country.
Look into their eyes and in the reflection
see the true you looking back . . . the real you.

In the name of humanity, cut the god damn strings!
We are human beings, we matter, we have value.
We are more than notches in political bedposts.

Let the you that has been smothered . . . breathe.
Let the you that has been beaten . . . heal.
Let the you that they have wanted fall away
to reveal the you, you were always meant to be.

Case Number

There is a sense of security that comes with things
These plastic mutations we tie ourselves to
Providing sense of purpose
Of ownership

Only to be stripped away
On a whim
Of a faceless entity
That operates through static

And the tin-shop sound
Of elevator music
Across the oceans
Making YOU wait

While they determine
If you are worth the risk

The Great Divide

She finds comfort in the wee lonely hours.
So often they don't understand . . . think her odd and slightly daft,
for she has grown so very tired of explaining.

It never gets her anywhere . . . any further,
to preach poetry to a soap-slicked politician
when the only constant is the truth weaved within her words.

She could shout it to the world
through grand and fantastic friendships
built on invisible ether, strange and unexpected connections spark!

She can hear them shouting back at her in understanding
over mountains and through the seas in sympathy of her plight, but
they are not there to hold her close and safe.

With the coming of blackest night.

With pen and paper she makes it through
to sincerely welcome a new day dawned.
Inspired by dream-scape and country-side.

But never by this thing they call love, this inspiration
that so many claim lends the best fuel for their pen.
She wonders of this, she writes of this.

As evening overtakes the sun
she knows that the time has come, the moment to decide,
but she wonders if there are words strong enough

to bridge this great divide.

The Pretty Things

I never cared for pretty things
Too precious did they seem
I was rather into oddities
Borderline obscene

I never cared for Barbie dolls
Nor skirts lest they were tore
I was fond of D&D
Where I could let my dragon roar

I never cared for hop and pop
Or ballads that would sit
I preferred screaming guitars
And moshing in the pit

I never cared for pink or rose
But revelled in the black
I preferred the skull and bones
With tattoos on my back

The pretty things that are for me
Cannot be built by man
I am one with native ways
A worshiper of land

A bleeding sunset, a purple storm
Are pretty things for me
A freak of nature, yes I am
But a pretty one indeed

Hat Rack

All these things that I have done.
All the people I have tried to be.
All the job descriptions . . .

complete lack of identity.
Tied to production levels.
Tied to another's

opinion of who and what
I should strive to become . . .
when I have always known.

But still you try to please.
Growing, shrinking,
according to what is needed.

Satisfaction gained for those
who are content to deny me
sustenance . . . soul food.

As long as they are happy.
As long as the quotas are met.
I will shape to fit.

As long as I can avoid
judgement raining down,
erasing . . .

my obviously invisible tears.

In Passing

Who knew that death could smell so sweet
Displayed on asphalt, August heat
No rose could hide that sickening scent
No carnation could prevent

This air that rises, a petal's rot
Where maggots crawl through flowerpots
And soil rises up to feed
Bringing beetles and centipedes

Life force spilled against the grey
A crimson stain on life's highway
Where machines bring hammers down
Divine plans at once turned round

Invaded by the mind's design
The end of breath, a lost bloodline
Taken down at peak of life
The mind of man cuts like a knife

And upon the rot in blackened eyes
The cutting scythe will claim its prize
A vessel of souls called back too soon
Dissolving now in death's cocoon

Back to the Earth she has been called
Though now on asphalt she lies sprawled
Upon the dust of histories
Wrapped 'round life's dark mysteries

Who knew that death could smell so sweet

The loss of life, upon soul's retreat
And trigger thoughts of awful things
This is the stuff that death does bring

About the Author

Residing on Canada's scenic east coast, Natasha Head has been expressing herself through poetry as far back as she can remember. She has recently published her first poetry collection, *Nothing Left to Lose*, and participated in the collaborative work *Inspiration Speaks*, both through Winter Goose Publishing. Her poetry blog, *The Tashtoo Parlour*, is a vibrant example of her work in progress, and she is proud to be a recurring host of the popular OpenLinkNight at the dVersePoets website.

Follow Natasha
Twitter: @Tashtoo
Become a friend: facebook.com/tashtoo
Become a fan: facebook.com/pages/The-Tashtoo-Parlour/134826696571007
Follow her blog: tashtoo.com